Moving
to
Delilah

Moving to
Delilah

Catherine
Owen

Freehand Books gratefully acknowledges the financial support for its publishing program provided by the Canada Council for the Arts and the Alberta Media Fund, and by the Government of Canada through the Canada Book Fund.

This book is available in print and Global Certified Accessible™ EPUB formats.

Freehand Books is located in Moh'kinsstis, Calgary, Alberta, within Treaty 7 territory and Métis Nation of Alberta Region 3, and on the traditional territories of the Siksika, the Kainai, and the Piikani, as well as the Iyarhe Nakoda and Tsuut'ina nations.

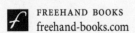

FREEHAND BOOKS
freehand-books.com

LIBRARY AND ARCHIVES CANADA CATALOGUING IN PUBLICATION
Title: Moving to Delilah / Catherine Owen.
Names: Owen, Catherine, 1971– author.
Description: Poems.
Identifiers: Canadiana (print) 20240286227
Canadiana (ebook) 20240286235
ISBN 9781990601583 (softcover)
ISBN 9781990601590 (EPUB)
ISBN 9781990601606 (PDF)
Subjects: LCGFT: Poetry.
Classification: LCC PS8579.W43 M68 2024 |
DDC C811/.54—dc23

Cover painting: *Coniferous Ruth* by Stacey Walyuchow
Author photo by Michael Belandiuk
Printed and bound in Canada

FIRST PRINTING

"what I dared not hope or fight for/is, in my fifties,
mine, a toft-and-croft/where I needn't, ever,
be at home to/those I am not at home with"

W.H. AUDEN
from "Thanksgiving for a Habitat," 1962

For Chris (1981–2010), who brought me to Edmonton first, and enabled me to buy Delilah, and to Michael, who joined me in the adventure from Winnipeg and has been part of me staying.

And for my parents, Gerald and Madeleine, who taught me to yearn for what a home means.

Prologues

Exodus: a directive

"For the sake of their financial future, young people should leave Toronto and Vancouver."
ROB CARRICK, *THE GLOBE AND MAIL*, NOVEMBER 2022

Young people should be prepared to leave Toronto & Vancouver,
the news story reports. Those who have simple dreams of land or castle,
these cities are not for you. If you want to make art, please go.
If you yearn to run a small and homey restaurant, a humble venue,
keep a backyard rooster, flee as fast as you can.
If you don't want to work six jobs at minimum wage
and live with your parents who were lucky enough to be young
during a different age, be gone. These cities are not for your kind.
We will ship in what we require from foreign lands to replace
your slaving and if you can't afford it, leave. If you're unable to
save forty years for a down payment or earn it fast through
drugs and crime, some fortunate lineage, or otherwise, then depart.
The city has no heart now, it can do without colour, light,
sound, without the young establishing families, without
children awakening the streets. Be prepared for the fact
that there is no future for you here, these lands where
the old and rich hoard the ocean or the lakes, they do not
share, they yield to none, all that means life in its fullness,
tomorrow in its possible, we have no need for you, so leave.

Getting There

Leaving New West

                    1. It was the time of the fires. Later

2. August, the truck

                              3. packed for its last long shift from an apartment on the coast

                4. to an old prairie

5. home, my father drove, my brother rode along to lift; we listened to Marshall

                            6. McLuhan podcasts as we left in the smeared

          7. dark, or was it Thomas Merton lectures, we were heading to Clearwater, a halfway point

8. with two cats, everything I owned, except for all I had lost.

*

Staying in Clearwater

It was a basic kind of motel where the cups are sealed in plastic. We went for
a walk and my father picked alleyway apples and my brother juggled them.
We ended up at a fancy restaurant in the middle of smoke. No one could
see the lake. Small German families disappeared off the dock while we ate
schnitzel and crab cakes with a relatively fine wine and espresso pie. There
was philosophy and puns and the haze never abated. It was a gentle kind of
apocalypse with warm family feelings. In the room, the cats were sleeping
on the scratchy duvet. We planned to hit the road again at eight. On the back
of the door, over the Emergency Exit plan in case of fire, my father hung his
Tilley hat.

*

Arriving in Edmonton

1. It was now midday. Once we had passed into the other

2. province, memories announced their perplexity. Why

3. was I returning? I fed the cats fishy sedatives, tried to recall

4. that owning a home was vital to me and eventually there we were and she was beautiful so

5. my other brother arrived and we all spent the night with pizza & beer

6. while beds were assembled, doors built, the lawn mown as the cats hid and then, they all

7. left, the truck grumbled back to the land of my birth, I waved & waved through

8. the flames like a child, then went inside to assume the extent of my dreaming.

The Voice

People ask – "How did you name your house?"
They mention Tom Jones, his song from '67
and I respond, "Why would I call my home
after a tune about a murdered woman?"
There was no reference point, no past
moniker to claim as the reason.
I just walked in, beneath the simple lintel,
and the walls spoke in a definite whisper,
"My name is Delilah" and there was no doubt.

Returning to Edmonton, nine years after

"You were ended/unexpectedly; what is only left of you is only me"
LUCIE BROCK-BROIDO

As if living on for a ghost some days.

At the Hotel Mac, I see him pretending to be chi-chi in the martini bar.

By the fire pit, we are at Red Deer River where he is cooking me tuna steaks

and laughing at how much he still loves me.

Down Jasper Avenue, somewhere, he was found dead in his truck.

Why did I move back.

Homage, not squander, I guess.

Putting what he left me into a thing of future.

A house of misery's beauty in a sense.

Never to regret, ever, at least some of it.

Yet spectral is part of the pact of this,

and lonely.

Identity

Edmonton is snow.
Vancouver, condos.
Is either a home, an alien zone, an ally?

Taking the ocean as my blood
doesn't mean a distant river
can't be kin too.

Monogamy of place,
is it ideal, the only notion,
must we be fixed to the singular?

Edmonton is oil,
Vancouver, yoga.
You see how language refuses

to say one thing as a summation,
and so adoring the ice is equally
as possible as the salt.

Two Homes: a corona

Your childhood home sings in your blood
as if it were a kind of wound, or mouth
and wherever you are, you duplicate
its rooms, straining to inhabit
those innocent comforts when a door
shut meant hours of deep time,
a meal around the table held sounds of chaos
& enough, when a box became a train
or puppet theatre or house and you
knew nothing of the costs, your parents' pain,
the years spent renovating all so
you could live in the seeming-magic of what was.

*

You could live in the seeming magic of what-was.
That's why you bought this older house –
most of your life thinking it would never be, Vancouverite,
priced-out, shifting from apartment to basement suite
to eventually a condo, but still knowing, for the future,
this wouldn't be sufficient. When your parents die,
the home, bereft of them, sold, what then? You,
nostalgia-sick, wouldn't endure. And so, to
save yourself, you found this place in Edmonton,
a house that matched the hominess of the walls
you grew up in, an edifice that had stood 115 years.
It surely would not, not now, or never, let you down.

*

It surely would not, not now (or never?) let you down.
The way the kitchen in your childhood home was hub,
orange & brown as the inside of a squash, complete
with Lazy Susan, spice racks, various implements
of self-sufficiency: a yoghurt maker, say, or fruit
dryer. Your mother wasn't a homebody but when
she was home, the kitchen steamed with bread, muffins,
that rich hippie granola baked with honey; there were
always squabbles about how much and for whom;
we all had our favourite and loathed mugs, plates, bowls
and beyond the sink where our dad rationed soap was a window
where the view was other homes and trees and the space between.

*

Where the view was other homes and trees and the space between
is what has now been lost in that house, the side cedars slashed
and the room around the homes packed in. But from where I am
now, I have it, the over-dipping limbs and large breaths
parting walls. Even if my kitchen has no children or endless
baking, it retains the core feeling of a gathering space, painted
ochre, teal and sea foam to replicate the coast or some exotic
realm of warmth, where crabs & starfish open drawers
and lights suspend their soft moons over an island crested
with plants. It's where the cats eat. And where meals
are dreamed. The galley kitchens in apartments lack
that generous breadth of possible nourishments.

*

That generous breadth of possible nourishments
isn't just food but the way you could fit around
the vast table, hundreds of years old, shipped from PEI
with the family's once, now vanished, money. The dining room
was where you learned conversation, manners, how you failed
with impatience, selfishness. Rules shielded you from randomness.
No, you couldn't rise from the table until all were done eating.
Yes, you could speak about nearly everything – which didn't
mean you were heard. Don't lean back in the green antique
chairs that always reminded you of your grandfather carving
the Christmas turkey – his one known-to-you job. The dining room –
a place to begin to inhabit the expanded world.

*

A place to begin to inhabit the expanded world –
your own dining room is instead a holding space,
not big enough by half to fit the massive ancestral table,
just a round of wood for four, though only two usually eat.
And who eats here much anyway? Mostly meals are on the lap
before a show or book, no need to mirror apropos
behaviour to children – cats indifferent – and so the dining
room keeps the antique tomes, some instruments, many
knick-knacks from the past: a bag of marbles, figurines from
Grade Four games, shells, rocks, a twist of sage – the closets
are hung with art, not coats, the back door wide to birds.
There is no one way of defining what a room is for.

*

There's no one way of defining what a room is for.
The living room is not where you truly lived, say,
but a communal space of mess, while it was your bedroom
that claimed the title of True Life Realm, from the age of six carving
you out a small square of self: that thinning rainbow carpet,
drapes in mid-century flowers, bookshelves you spent hours at,
picking out your Pearl S. Buck, Tolkien, Dickinson, clicking
the spines back in – satisfying sound! Then, as a teen, this room
was poster land and a pit, sometimes, of self-examinations gone wrong
at the six-toggle mirror, within diaries hidden in the bedside dresser.
Ten years, the same four walls shaped your dreams.
Since then, you've always asserted your need for a room.

*

Since then, you've always asserted your need for a room.
Even in tiny apartments, demarcating a space and now,
in this house you have the studio of your dreams, part the somber
chamber of making, part the silly museum of childhood where
a desk, printer, the necessities, share the space with an array of books
from Mother Goose to John Ashbery, and shelves are lined with sand
dollars, Cuban pesos, old dolls, Polaroids. A citrus rug tossed on the floor,
a John Deere logo painted on the closet door (there from before, yes,
but too quirky to cover!). The sixty-year-old Christmas cactus
you call Charlotte, lanyards, calendars, instruments – each
morning your routine of coffee, thoughts and words –
when you look around you feel at home, allowed, contained.

*

When you look around you feel at home, allowed, contained –
as you did even outside the house your father built,
crouching on the front steps with cereal as birdsong entered you
or on the cedar-ragged patch of grass beneath the tallest
trees in the world, bark your small legs grappled with, constellated
with sweet beads of sap, the varying swings or slides hung
or propped up, the rock in the corner of the low berm you knew
had been there since the beginning of time. The yard was another
room. It defined the house as not just object but space.
Entering it you could connect with neighbours, witness street life,
be a fragment in the mosaic of the road as cars blurred by.
The garden, inextricable from the dream entire.

                    *

The garden, inextricable from the dream entire.
Not that you are a gardener, per se, being too enamoured
with weeds for this rigour, but that you wished to replicate
expanse, the options of earth, announce that yes,
there could be a vegetable patch there and here fruit trees,
the knowledge that at least the lilac would return, those
magnolias and clumps of wild chives amid the paving stones.
Home being not only inside but the surround of air and green,
the puttering made possible in dirt you pretend you own,
all the reveries of what you might do to the garage or shed
or deck or fence to make them yet another expanse of
your weird yearnings. But are they?

                    *

Your weird yearnings. But are they?
Is this much nostalgia strange in a world
bent on erasure, elision? The way a house there
for only 45 years has taken on such permanence
in your brain as if you were still a child who says
there was no earth before me and I can't imagine death.
O but I can, now, my parents old and moved
downstairs and the tenuous reign over the home left to other
family members who may not keep it once they are gone.
So you know, in your lifetime, it will be lost, your father's
blueprint for a vision, your mother's warm touches.
This – why you wanted a house to call your own.

*

This – why you wanted a house to call your own.
Not that true replication is possible; there is only you,
your boyfriend, cats, after all, as shifting inhabitants
but the idea of home is held by this over-a-century
manse, the shape of it prevails, has through so many
weathers & owners, booms & busts, and thus you can
rely on it, you must, as what is yours now, or an
approximation of, in these years left you, a consolation,
a solace, if never a turning back of youth's clock, still
the hope that your dreaming has its parts, chapters,
a form that turns a chaotic story calmer though
your childhood home sings (always) in your blood.

Dedication for a Home

When I bought this house I wanted it to be my house alone.

I wanted to own it. Not in that way – oh I know no one really owns anything,

or that I yearned to dominate a piece of land and extirpate its weeds & natives

& irrational elements, to tame it, or that I don't know a dead man's money helped

to buy it and it was his wish and so he can claim ghost ownership

or that I don't know I will die and the house pass on to other wild dreamers

or else be eaten by a machine and its drifting cells transform into this era's abode:

shiny & cold & new.

When I bought this house I wanted to own it like I've learned to own my body,

so I could say no to any non-agreed shifting of boundaries, so I could define

where the art would hang, the books slot, each knick-knack assume its magical place,

so no one, no man could say to me again we're done because I'm a wrong

kind of woman and with his hands or feet and voice kick me out, so that

I could only lose on my own terms, or close to them.

When I bought this house, I recalled all the women who have been barred from ownership,

who have lived solely under the sway, the pain of others, and wanted to honour them by keeping

this house in my name and only leaving it when my own machine came and my cells said

let's move on out into the world.

The House

Delilah

"we are together at last, though far apart"
JOHN ASHBERY

You wanted me to have this house and I always
      listen to the dead,
though there are things you didn't account for of course,
      as in that I
would be alone, not actually with you, in the home
      and that thus
the winters would be longer, more difficult, money less,
      no car
and so harder to return to my family on the coast
      where the heart
in me is formed of salt & cedar. Or are these things
      I didn't consider?
Though I
      couldn't be other than here,
in the present, we are now having another
      kind of harsh relationship,
and there will be struggles to honour your name,
      your gift
(at least you can't die again, there is this.)

Salt Box Special

When he shared this fact – the Newfie who knew
that all such homes built between 1860 and 1920
back East or even, obviously, on the prairies
were common, named after the shape of salt
as sold in tiered boxes, so that the front view
looks capacious, when the back is only one floor
above a slanted roof, built in whatever wood
was available for the speed of the build
and shaped like this to save taxes –
I was a bit insulted, shamed as if I had bought
the lame designs of a Vancouver Special, those
typical cookie-cutter frames I grew up with.

But, of course, after 115 years, the Salt Box Specials
are rare, and testament to the toughness of materials,
the ingenuity of settlers who wanted solidity, the affordable,
and even some slight majesty, their homes mimicking
containments of what flavours, what preserves.

History

Since 1905, when there was nothing else
around it, just grass and saplings in aching
distance from the river, how many lived
in this place, maybe a hundred, surely in
115 years, and yet I am only oddly beset
by you, your energy that seems to float
in the grain, tremble in the wainscoting,
even hold the weeds that aura the old,
enduring foundations.
But who can be open to all?
The mind, gut, heart, selects its ghosts
or is chosen in some strange way to bear
the passages of unsettled, unsettling love.
I am here like someone bidden, in haste
to meet a spouse, only to discover, again

that yes, they are dead, not dead, found, lost.

Forms of Knowledge: The Census

That you will never trace the faces of all this house's inhabitants.

That there were years the place was vacant, often amid the evacuation of wars, the economy's harsh crash common to prairie provinces.

There were soldiers who lived here, the first locatable year, 1915, after the Hotel Mac was built, the railway, but when wagon tracks still scored their ancient paths through what would soon be Packingtown.

That there were then insurance agents, labourers for Canada Dry, carpenters, as many as four at a time though the children, if any, weren't listed, ghosts of this compendium, only numbers of adults and their sources of employment mattering.

That the house used to bear a much lower street number before the area's amalgamation with Strathcona, and also, because everything was less.

But there are ten years remaining unaccounted for, that history is not a smoothly recorded progression; Eliot and Woolf may have been composing masterpieces on one continent while here, 1905 was brush and mud and only the beginnings of a small and tenuous empire of oil.

That the slaughterhouses came before this, slabs of meat layered in cases and shipped off.

That this house once had no other houses around it, the initial abode, or else, every other shred of tangible evidence of this time has been torn down and somehow, your house continues to hold a whole other era's unfolding.

That your name, too, will be added to that list of the dead.

The Guest Who Didn't Leave

for Michael, five years on, final Airbnb tenant

They were never extra rooms to me but still, an influx of funds required,
a month post-move, I rented, on a temporary basis, spaces

to short-term travellers: two backpackers from Bern, a couple who
complained about pilling towels then, madness, five young Quebeckers

in the basement, the weekend an eternity of je m'excuse, smoke awaft,
alarms set off, naked relay races before, even worse, a reckless hot-knifer,

a Beijing family seeking refuge, a Turkish cartographer who prowled the floors
deeming there was never enough space and thus, could he sprawl?

At the end of six weeks, he arrived, this man from Winnipeg, bassist
with an itinerant spirit who slapped cash in my hand, dropped his bags,

took off for the road. Ahhhh, perfection. Solitude in combo with bill payments.
What could be better. Then he returned and, amicable, became partner. The ad dissolved.

Uncoveries: haibuns on renovating a garage

1
Barn Door

It was a door in the roof. As planks calved from the ceiling with pry bars, an old slab slipped, descended to cement. It was a gate from the sky. What had it once shut? Hinge-less but with a thin metal handle pressed into its furred wood, slats solid. Imagined a shed, a barn, a magical trap, some faded rural scene of a pre-'50s Alberta Ave, but perhaps it was just a stopper for a dog or a side passageway into the yard. Having little to go on, we make up the details. It was a door from the sky. It was a gate in the roof. Blake's angels would have something to say about this.

> Square of once-forest
> What world did you close against?
> Simple gate; strange place.

2
Building Permit

Once, the basement was crawl-space cinderblock. Until 1956 when the decision was made to raise the foundations to ten feet tall and pour cement walls, insulated, sump-pumped, small-windowed sufficient for not solely storage but for roughed-in rooms, unfinished still but serviceable. Even the tallest can stand without agony in the space that contains a range of this-n-that: drums, a treadmill, chairs, a dartboard, tins of leftover paint on high plastic shelves. Inside an empty cupboard we found the permit to build, its back scarred with tack marks, front bearing the contractor's name and a list of tasks to be checked off. None were. Or else the yellowed progression of time had swallowed the ticks that claimed the foundation (yes) had been finished or the frame (yes), the base (yes). We can see the evidence, the proof it was, yet the record is gone.

> How much we rely
> On the writing in the sand
> Near a hungry sea.

3
Oil Cans

Some time in history this was an automotive shop, hooked up to a defunct power
source, oil fresh on the floor, tools on various hooks until that ghost moved on and
the wires were sliced, the garage returned to a space slower with purpose. Below, in
a banged-up cupboard a Timmy's tin of nails, yet in the rafters, much older, Castrol
containers, their bright logos bearing the elemental colours of poison but empty,
rusted about the edges, they have taken on the aura of art, a useless moving beauty
of once-garbage, the discarded, and I could fill them full of autumn's last blooms.

> These hollow vessels
> Holding their moment of time
> Made lovely by rust.

4
Welder's Mask

Grey plastic shield with the back strap eroded, front panel a rectangle of glass,
alien as a diver's face, a mask against fire, this dark garage once ripped with sparks
as welds held vehicles together, ditched on departure in the half-attic among grills,
casters, nails and a crushed lawn chair from mid-century camp-outs, its husk,
leant against the wall, protecting no flesh for over half a century, only a medieval
knightly guise waiting to become a modern fossil.

> You, the mechanic
> Of Alberta Avenue, lit
> Up by this finding.

5
Wallet with Photographs

In the archives of who lived here then, during the transitional '50s, there is no
mention of him, Paul Deran, and yet, in the yanked-down roof of the dim garage,
we find his wallet: once-brown, chamois-soft leather made by English Manor,
stiffened by over 60 years of abandonment inside the rafters of a lost automotive

shop. Who were you, Paul? The cards left in cracked plastic sheaths suggest a
farmer (Union of Agricultural membership, No. 329, Exp Oct 31st, 1955) who
took unemployment in the off-season (Insurance Commission ID). Nothing else.
Except seven photographs of the same woman with gently marcelled locks, mid-
century cheekbones, a red glamour of lipstick, in passport pictures, sloped against
doorways, standing, eyes strained and smiling, at some wild beach far from here
(this is myself at Westlock, reads the penciled inscription on the back, so very faint).
You loved her. That is evident. And must have felt devastated when these traces of
her went missing. Paul Deran, I give them back to you now, long-dead lover, farmer.
These words are all I have.

> Identity cards,
> Photos of a beloved:
> Life's tiny wallet.

6
Wasps' Nests of Varying Sizes

The first one was under the eaves and fell with a soft hiss in a rainstorm, unfolding
its news on the pavement, a wealth of squinting larvae, snitched up by magpies or
peregrines. The second two or three were small and neat, tidy fragile globes that fit
in the palm, tiny wasp dreams of spherical silences, emptied now. The last one was
immense, wedged inside the garage behind slats of planks, layered and combed for
generations, a thick, dry filter glued to the wall where, pried out by nails, it revealed
wasps dead in each cell, some arrested as they flew as if by poison, others fetal,
and beneath, a midden of wasps, handfuls of workers stilled in their ancient
archives of paper.

> So many creatures
> Within our edifices
> Living in their pasts.

The Pipe

1

They have beautiful words for it – the plumbers – decay.
That ancient water pipe, cast iron with massive joists and a core of lead,

lumbering from roof to basement, bringing our twisting water
back to earth for 116 years. The rot? They call it blossoms.

Rust in small dangerous buds on the eroded surface, promising
to split, flower into a disaster of flood.

Is there anything we can do to stop it? Replace segments,
understand our history, hope the bouquet never assembles.

2

The pipe's dragged out in chunks, heavy lengths of iron that spent
over a century serpenting through these walls,

carrying water for all our hungers and losses
and now is only a cumulus of rust in split sections on the deck.

Look, the plumber says, *here's a fissure like a brook, there,*
holes large as dimes, how it hasn't widened to the size of a flood,

I don't know, but you've been lucky. So, in gratitude, we plan
to plunge each short shaft in the soil, deep enough to become

old pots for blossoms, the pipes eventually containing gardens,
still, in another form, allowing life.

The house becomes

The house becomes another body
or your own, othered out,
a wood-and-cement flesh

much older than yours and so able
to offer endurance to the everyday,
an eros of endlessness in the now.

The house becomes another mind
or your own, outed in its reveries of colour,
every wall affixed to dreams, all the furniture

emblazoned with memory, a spectacular
denizen, a small-realms traveller.
The house – not just an edifice,

an address you signed for, an agreement
with time – but the wild-tame you slipped
inside yourself – said my thing-person,

my companion-shell.

1905/2020: linked haikus

The hopeful built you.
Before even the first train
smudged into town, not

yet a capital
city, until that year's end,
1905 pre-

housing boom, mostly
snow & mud & that hoping
it would all soon grow

and now, the hopeful
stay, knowing jobs are few, that
oil has fled – but then

was knowing ever
the dream, moving into this
prairie home? No, like

those who built you it
is hope that keeps me here, but
not for certainty.

1905: Four Headlines Each Month on Page One of the *Edmonton Journal* as Tiny Love Letters

January 13th: Apples, Apples. / Stoves, Stoves.

Pay attention to what installs itself in you.
All the meadows, the varietals.
Heat arrives in many guises, no, just one.
What can I say that would feed you for a lifetime?

January 20th: Are you Wise on Hot Water Bottles? / Woodsmen, Attention!

Why would you think this a consideration.
Even in the bigness of winters.
Your provisions to enter these forests:
An awl or two, or was it awe, endless.

February 1st: Why go Blind? / Homemade Candy

There may be a choice to keep seeing.
The way your irises are reflected in teacups.
When I glimpse you sometimes I'm gumdrop, a slow
Sucked thing, fashioned from the boil & stir of your mouth.

February 11th: Valentines are more Popular than ever. /
You can scarcely find a Present More Acceptable to a Lady than a Nice Desk.

In the wilderness, paper hearts are scarce, darling.
We shall live in the meat-packing district after all.
Lug it up the stairs towards my sanctum.
The place I practise my cursive pain.

March 16th: Marmalade Oranges! / Your Money has a String to it.

Anything redolent of the old country a vague comfort.
The zing of citrus in chunks on toast; you, first light
In the morning beneath comforters, leashed to me
But not like dollars, not, at any rate, from fear.

March 24th: Good Lumber. / Lace Curtains.

Can you have one without the other? The former,
Important, manly, a solid outline of days,
But raw, leaving you in the wild of dead trees
Without the filigreed coverings – pretended, delicate, privacy.

April 3rd: The Perfect Home requires Perfect Plumbing. / Corset sale still on.

I guess there's otherwise no way to woo you –
I can't say go out back, all my gifts are structure, entire.
And then will I receive the cut-rate accoutrements of night?
A changing of shapes to the discomforts of touch.

April 22nd: Killed by Yard Engine. / Ladies Fancy Collars and Belts for Easter.

When it's nearly the first train ever, who's aware?
The thrill of wheels & steam, the addendums of empire, arriving.
Who doesn't want to seem attired for the unseen?
The latest bands around your waist, your pale neck.

May 2nd: Curtain Stretchers. / Good Solid Plumbing.

What you need for your wet lace thoughts. A strong
Extension as they dry, then return to your naked windows.
It can't be stressed enough. The power of internal connectors.
Behind every decent human are lengths & lengths of pipe.

May 9th: Rhubarb: 4 lb for 25c. / Don't wait till the Flies come.

That fruit with the toxic leaves. Once it seeds –
Pies & violence everywhere! We're told to have a full
Pantry before proposing love, but I can hear the swarm
Coming from the North Sask River, and want you now.

[no newspapers were printed in June, July or August]

September 6th: Going to Build? / You are Hit Hard.

Everyone's looking for the same thing – how to
Make a land hold them, repeat – stay awhile – but
When is love that simple? Out of nowhere, the heart
Gets in the ring, goes down, stumbles through its door of blood.

September 12th: Struck Large Gusher. / Slightly Injured about the Face.

The beginnings of this one horse, one plow, one egg
In a basket town. The drama of it drawing you anyway.
No one escapes this minor wounding – approaching the machines
Too intimately, begging they serve as human balm.

**October 5th: Jan McDiarmid went to Wetaskiwin this morning. /
Have you Bought your Winter Underwear yet?**

If only the news was – you moved me to joy last
Night or this afternoon I took a trip inside your soft passages.
But we are always thinking towards the cold here,
Doing business, layering up, getting on with it.

October 14th: Good Coal. / The Last Preserving Fruit of the Season.

Yes, we dream constantly about keeping warm here,
I don't deny that: stocking up, shovelling hard.
Still, how can I forget my final feeling, that sweet taste
Held behind glass, so that summer revisits you in the snow.

November 11th: Fell down a Well. / Storm Windows.

Does this imply – don't look into the depths anymore?
Between this & that: stone, moss, the dark.
You can count on the instability of weather at least.
Install layers of glass, keep watch from within.

November 28th: What about Furs? / Wound is Fatal.

Wrap yourself in all the attributes of animals.
Hibernate wisely, dear. Life likes to thump
Us where it counts and some encounters
Carry on after, some repeat until the end.

December 19th: Bibles-Poets. / A Hot Time.

Even in this new prairie town, we provide the range:
The God to the gods, first love to the fadings.
Economies burning in their race to claim
And what we know always: that soft fire in the mind.

December 31st: Slaughter Sale of Holiday Goods. / Evolution Of a Modern Daily.

Wanting the baubles of a week ago – cheap things
Bought after the feast – knowledge on hooks,
Swinging in the future of meat. But we've learned, haven't we?
What was it again? The new year lays out its font & waits.

The Roof

Protection is an archeological book now.
The initial page an original shake layering

above the former lath & plaster walls,
solid wood that lasted the first 40 years

before the second chapter of red shingles
was overlaid prior to that '50s basement raising

and then, sometime 20 years ahead
of your arrival, black shingles were nailed down.

The inspector told you on purchase that it
was time to replace the crisping squares, lifting

their edges after so many winters, and now you have,
with metal designed to last forever, turning your 1905

home into the ghost of a robot pagoda, slightly
futuristic, somewhat industrial, but wholly sealed

and hopefully the last layer, that final page
in all the assemblages of love.

Six Words

Last night the only home I'd owned was sold
suddenly, for no especial reason, in a dream:
cash exchanged, the sign fixed in the garden
and what I'd thought was an always-home
had become a thing of wood & stone, a house.
No, I warned the movers, you won't get me to leave.

Since I was a child I've been stubborn, wouldn't leave
when told, but they insisted, your dream home was sold,
you have no choice, and down the road, another house
awaits, one that may be equal to this loss, a different dream
of permanence and joy. They didn't know how I defined home:
old, well lived-in, colourful and set in a garden

of happily ragged proportions, the kind of garden
where you might find dandelions and roses, irises within leaves,
raked into a heap beneath the apple tree, the type of home
where the owner's signature holds, won't be sold
as if it were just part of the market, that anonymous dream
where homes are only things, structures, mere houses,

houses upon houses, their stock rising & falling, houses & houses
shuffled like heavy cards on an agent's table with their disposable gardens,
their erasable lineage. Death will take all this (I know) with its dream
of darkness, the sharp way it points from its shadows, you leave
and you leave too, your possessions, your hopes, all inevitably sold
by someone else, o the joke of it, your hahaha home –

that you would imagine, for an instant, a permanent home
when you are essentially water and your home a house
that, in the night, was unceremoniously, behind your back, sold:
the walls, floors, ceilings; the stairs, doors, windows; the gardens
all dispatched and you informed by the Great Mover to leave
and was this or was it not only a terrible dream,

just another reverie of an anxious mind, a dream
that denies the thing you crave, a place named home,
this solid symbol of self you never have to leave,
though time will remind you of object facts, that this is a house,
not a resurrection-machine and that perfect garden?
It's not a land that can't be sold

and yet your house, your garden, won't yet be sold
in this holy dream of home you refuse to leave.

The Book Box: 12 months in 13 parts

for Gerald Owen

1 July (early)

On the VIA train between Vancouver and Edmonton, my father
checks a suitcase in which layered slabs of wood: sides, back, a
pointed roof, are slid in flat as heavy garments, telling the porter
it's a building project, a little library for his daughter's
prairie home. The blankness on his face at the weight of the case,
this weird gesture of love.

2 July (later)

A day or two of touristy sojourns and Dad wants to build. Hammering
the pieces together is a simple recipe, but then, how to plant
it in the earth, ensure it doesn't topple over with its three
shelves of books? He settles finally on a six-foot stake that
he handsaws out into a slot for the box to sit. Then digs
with a small trowel a hole two feet deep and wedges
the whole creation in, bracing it against the picket fence.
Solid. The glassed-in door first held by an elastic, then, better,
a magnet. The roof, tiles like a tiny version of the house behind it.
And now, to the filling, the texts.

3 August

My own library, relatively capacious and wanting to retain its largesse
can't be the main source. Occasionally, a disappointment
will be ditched or poetry books past review left but the tomes
mostly come from passersby or a coffee shop down the street
with its own little collection in the back beyond the espresso

machine. Or presses that offload their excess in boxes, shipped,
or authors, tired of stacks of titles, willing now to send them away,
free. I get too many Ann Rule or worse, and need to weed
regularly, but the worst are Bibles or the Book of Mormon or
Hare Krishna pamphlets. These get bagged up and sometimes
just tossed.

4 September

By later summer, I make a sign, typed, printed on a small sheet,
cut out and taped behind the glass that reads: this is a pagan
literary book box. No utter trash or religious tracts. Please.
Then a smiley face. No offence meant but keep your gods
to yourself.

5 October

It takes some time for neighbours to notice the library behind
the still-leaved lilac tree: double-takes as they stride past on dog
walks, a slowed-down car, one small boy on a bike crying out to
his mother – "look, a little library!" Through I prefer to call it
a book box, as this has greater accuracy and no lending implied plus, just –
take what you want, drop off if you can, come back for more.

6 November

The demographic: women of a certain age, often. Alone
or slowing their partners down to take a peek in the middle of a stomp.
Sometimes kids whinging to "see what's there!" Once a young
couple standing awhile by the open door each picking a text,
comparing their selections. The engagement is what I enjoy the most:
with books, each other. Those who burn past without even a side
glance make me wonder what kind of people they are.

7 December

The first real snows start and with them a glut of romance
novels, bought cheap from the Shoppers and stuffed into the shelves
after. I leave a sampling; the rest get recycled. Keeping a kind of order
is a daily pleasure: bottom shelf, non-fiction and kids' books, low
enough so they can reach them solo; middle – all the trashiness
I can handle; top, the classics and where it never is in actual bookstores,
poetry, pre-eminent, allocated priority and yes, it goes faster
than I'd imagined – review copies, randoms, the entire shipment
of Brick Books titles, quickly disappeared by one obsessed reader –
I think – taking the opportunity to take all types of poems within.

8 January

Gifts, in the book box, aren't limited to Christmas.
When I see the card taped to the glass, I initially think,
a lost cat notice again or some other neighbourhood need:
bottle drives, pancake breakfasts. But it's a card depicting
a nest full of eggs and a newly hatched chick squawking how
my library is "awesome" and thanks for my "sense of ha-ha."
They may mean my sign or how I arrange the genres; it
doesn't matter. The library is a vector of care now, noticing,
bond. Over the next few months, occasional gifts appear:
a mug writ Caticorn, two smooth crystals, a teenager's
notebook of scrawled stymied love poems, making me feel
that no time has elapsed since me at fifteen and now.

9 February

This, the hunger that offers hope –
the sight of a lone man, stopping
in a snowstorm – at least 30 below –

47

and taking the moments he needs
to select a book, drifts becoming texts
on the shelves, before sliding his selection
inside his thick coat and, angling against
the flakes, walking on.

10 March

A strange pandemic begins and libraries shut,
bookstores close but the small box with its three
welcoming shelves stays open, furnishing need.

At times, it's nearly gutted, there's such a desire
to stuff the long hours with words, then, it's
replenished and again all the genres flit from their spots,

poetry, the most, I notice. Also there's Puzzle Lady
who never fails to arrive twice a week with her
Danielle Steel and jigsaws of pastoral scenes.

They're soon gone too.

11 April

The door left wide, I see that someone has ripped my paper sign
that asks plainly for nil propaganda and no bottom-of-the-barrel.
Shreds stick to lengths of tape and we wonder at the anger's source.
Within minutes, another sign is printed out, the smiley face again and
now the word "Respect," the phrase "Read On," is stuck back
to the door. As often, the object of attack was not what is, but
likely, ire at another part of society telling them what to do, my sign
not to domineer, but to minus the Books of Mormon I feel like
ditching in the snow.

12 May

The best, and especially during isolation's time, is working
in the garden and, from behind the arbour of peonies, seeing
neighbours stop at the box, chat, pick a title and then, spying
me there with my shovel, talking awhile. Compost Woman wants
to thank me for the pagan nature of my collection and Cycling
Family asks what I like to read, myself. Strangest
is when a toothless lady crosses the street to bark,
"Can I say something?" I shrink a bit but then
she carries on, "I love your book box. Great stuff.
Use it often," drawing me taut by my judgement, relieved.
Always, repartee involves the tale of how my dad constructed
it, as, for twenty years now, the story of how he built the Al
Purdy podium has been shared – these things matter, the building,
filling, then creating narrative from it all.

13 June

This has not been an easy land to re-enter, the people
less the issue than the topography, weather, the dearth
of jobs. But, even in solitude, this house, garden and book box
bring uncountable bounties to the usual everyday and watching
neighbours lingering just beyond the door, talking about
the arrayed titles, laughing, gives me the strange hope I need.
Yesterday, two young girls said anxiously, after gushing,
"O I love this one!" – "but this is a library so it means you have
to return the book after." And "No," I reassured from beneath
the giant shadow of the scent-heady lilacs, "take them, keep them
forever if you need." The book box being a small nook
of freedom, the unknown in the familiar, the comforts of childhood,
a meeting place, a memorable embrace, a thread.

The Rescue

Of course, a storm.
The report speaking sun for days
so we removed the book box door, puzzled
as it had become by years of rain eroding
its particle board, tarnishing the plexiglass,
determined to fix it during this perfect, dry time.

The books would be fine, bared in their stacks
of Perrault fairytales, Danielle Steel, gluten-free
cookbooks and old Lorna Crozier castoffs.
Then, five a.m., the bang-crack of the unexpected,
should-have-known, and down in my dressing gown
and un-slippered feet, to the street with a recycling bin

to save what remains from the relentless rain until
the door returns to enclose, protect, offer something like hope to the world.

Conversation with the City Archivist regarding evidence of my house in 1905

There's little here.
If you've already tried that.
I mean it's worth a shot.
I guess.
I've been at this job 30 years.
Let me tell you.
They weren't careful with their records.
No aerial photos until 1923.
Directories? Post-1908 and partial.
If you're lucky.
Did you want heritage designation?
That's tricky.
They were terrible at keeping things.
Even permits were lax.
Or else not left to us at all.
It was only dirt then.
A rush to build for gold
& skins & oil before the war's
giant crash.
They didn't value a paper trail.
But you're welcome to sit awhile,
Burn your eyes on microfiche, work
Backward to 1905, have a gander as to what can be
Pieced together.
It won't be much.
I've worked here half my life.
There isn't a lot to find.
They were just living you see.
Not leaving behind.

City Archives: Trying to Find the Builder

The real ledgers are gone.
All that's left is lodged in a reel,
operable by arrows, switches.

For hours, numbers click past:
Lot 6, 7, Block A, Plan 7064AH
is what you seek but can't locate.

There must have been a record
at some point to prove the date,
the year, who sought to build in that space.

Now there are missing pages, smudges, cribbed,
incomprehensible script of who
& where, no Carey Street at all, just Clara

& Clarke, mostly illegible, only the what:
residence, dwelling, stable, church,
store, pool room, shack.

Constraints & Melancholia, 2020

Some mornings, I just want my land back – of course,
why would I lie – here already, in mid-November, two

feet of white and that cheating sunshine – all light and no
promise you can sit beneath its rays, stroll distances in comfort.

I miss the rain because I know it and the streets, how they curve,
where they dead-end, fear lessened there and of course the ease increased,

of reaching mountains, forests, the ocean. I never realized
how spoiled I was until I bought this house on the prairies

and it has had to become – almost entirely right now – my topography, my jailer,
my landscape, my haven, my reality, my world.

The Christmas Cactus

Only the old receive names:
the house, now 117, is instantly christened Delilah,
while this plant, passed on from several maternal generations,
over 60 years of age, is called Charlotte.

Every December, or almost, she blooms, and here,
on the prairies, the contrast is extreme:
snow beyond, a minus world, and within,
the misnamed cactus, without a desert inclination

for dry, spurts delicate hearts of darker & lighter
pink, five-folded, with fritillary petals and a scarlet tip.
Willy-nilly she bursts and for a few weeks,
on the early-century desk by the studio window,

the tropics attend my winter, a kind of light,
recollection's other, a whisper towards spring.

Will your cats be in this book?

Ramiro, the teller, reassessing my mortgage rate,
up a fearsome three percent from 2018, chats
my anxiety down by talking about his cats,
how since he came to Canada a decade ago,
he's become one of those people for whom
home and gato are inseparable and I realize
felines are so enmeshed with my life, this current
quartet of black & orange beasts, aged twelve to three,
with their indifferences and kibbles, skirmishes
and naps, cuddles and stews that I nearly forgot
to write their mews into a poem, so thanks
for reminding me, Lynn Tait.

The Built-in Bookcase

Renovations: mainly inwards, unimpressive
like plumbing, electrical, the private essential,
or visible, as with the roof, but still banal,
lacking the zing of the unique.

When you planed white oak, then black matte stained it; when
it became solid boxes nine feet high up one whole
wall, hammered in hard, fitted with trim, this was different.
The lath & plaster spines straightened into the centre,

a modern casement for old books, collections arching half a century
now and beyond, the span in the middle an eventual
brace for a ladder. How fast it would be filled, would hold,
not only a library, but that weird bond now, to home,

to that bad vagabond of the heart,
saying at the longest last, stay, stay.

The Home Performance Series: a recipe

1 Turn up the room to 350 degrees.

2 Mise en place: brief & printed bios, various snacks, wine glasses (washed!), chairs, arrayed.

3 Greet the guests. Spread them in a single layer around the space. Ensure they possess all the

4 liquids they need. Oil the air with fine chatter.

5 Introduce the piece de resistance first: The Al Purdy Podium, built by your father in 1995:

6 it's green, contains a shelf for the poet's fabled beer, a slanted path for his foot and solid

7 sides to grip while reciting sex & death. Signed by Joe Rosenblatt for extra flavour.

8 Combine all the arts you can, as many artists you can cram, and mix well: poets, fictionistas,

9 painters, musicians. Maybe a dash of dancer now and again. Somehow, they will all fit on this

10 parchment-lined sheet of time.

11 You'll know the show is done when laughter sheens, applause pops, conversation crisps,

12 each has taken their turn on the gentle grill (and now perhaps can sell a book, a CD?)

13 Bid adieu to this delicious irreverent feast. Clean.

The Garden

In My Back Garden in September

The society of birds before seven,
when an edge of crescent moon evanesces
over the slowing garden, tomatoes sensing
winter in their skins and cider apples softening
into a thin wine scent instead.

First finch, chickadee, sparrow, before the gronk
of blue jay and the plasticky tweaks magpies sound
settling on wires beneath the random crows,
a gull so far from the sea. Who can bring you
back to me. No one. Everything.

September

So early
this year
the snow
is like losing
you was
one day
grass thickening
above the loam
the next
white annulling
everything
but then
death is always
like this
no matter
how long you repeat
to yourself
the winter
of all I love
will come
when you wake
to so many
flakes of cold
shifting the landscape
you still utter
O!
as if this final season
was a time
no one
told you about
or you thought
just for you
there would be
immunity
from the ice
instead of always
too early
this snow.

Forms of Knowledge: Winter

That snow squeaks in extreme cold.

That boots placed on the floor of the vestibule will freeze to the lino overnight.

That mice will enter the rooms at the first dip of December
and be quickly dispatched by the cats.

Birds, even the smallest, that they will continue to attend the routine of seeds,
despite how, at minus 40, lungs refuse to balloon, fingers pang instantly, nostrils
stick; they, with their infinitesimal feathers, remain to squabble over grain at the
weighed-down-with-drifts feeder.

That you must learn to stay inside, to draw on those inner resources some mothers
once counselled were available, to recall that only the boring are bored.

That when you venture out regardless and slip hard on the sidewalk rinks you
must blame no one but yourself or else just accept the slides as the price of living
here and descend gracefully like a starfish of ice.

That the neighbourhood, so many months under white, will be the quietest you
have ever lived in, the old house holding its knowledge of over a century of waiting
for spring's fast passage, then summer's slower steeping of heat.

That winter is a place you will relearn every year, without guile and with gumption.

That snow outlines everything in bright relief, makes the world pop, as it did when
you were a child.

Seasonal Pantoum, Slightly Tinged

Flakes fall in their requisite repetitions
The grey day opens up and becomes white
There is one narrow window to watch the world from
And inside there is winter, continuing in the brain

The grey day opens up and becomes white
Slowly, the porte cochere, the transom hide
And inside there is winter, continuing in the brain
It's the accretions you don't witness that hurt

Slowly, the porte cochere, the transom hide
The last century is gradually erasing itself
It's the accretions you don't witness that hurt
All the childhoods that pile up in the dark

The last century is gradually erasing itself
Your grandparents with their routines became silly
All the childhoods that pile up in the dark
What's the point of making the duvet, winding the clock?

Your grandparents with their routines became silly
Why flip the wooden blocks or go to church on Sundays?
What's the point of making the duvet, winding the clock?
Death, as a rule, arrives anyway

(Why flip the wooden blocks or go to church on Sundays?)
The family quickly shrinking to its newest components
Death, as a rule, arrives anyway
Shaking its maracas or with black slippers on

The family quickly shrinking to its newest components
Death saying Hey you, Hasta la Vista, Avaunt
Shaking its maracas or with black slippers on
As a white bird sings from the whitening branch

Death saying Hey you, Hasta la Vista, Avaunt
There is one narrow window to watch the world from
As a white bird sings from the whitening branch
Flakes fall in their requisite repetitions

The Adopted Garden: Late May

1

After the final snowfall when I am sure
(no, how can I be) that the earth will not
seize itself to ice for the next few months (anyway),
I assess the raised boxes, slices of paving stones,

the front swoop of landscaped mulch and rock
and do not know what will come up –
those inches of green, are they weeds or bulbs?
I have to wait for someone else's dream.

2

Raking randomly, tossing the unprocessed soil
from the compost (still raddled with eggshells,
pits) onto the unpromising beds, yanking
out the chance that this plant isn't supposed

to grow though, in the end, I don't really
know the difference.

3

A rain and I return to definite evidence
of what was once planned: honeysuckle,
raspberries gangling on the path, the shaggy
physiques of peonies and are those irises

on the edge of unfurl? I love the garden
they made, the former owners of this ancient
prairie home, but I want to fit myself in too –
a shout of tomatoes, that hum herbs make

and definitely sunflowers singing, "I've arrived,
somewhere else, and am somehow, hanging on."

Sonnet on My End-of-the-Season Garden

The sog that summer was seemed ensmalling;
perhaps I would have nothing to harvest, or the ghosts
only of what could have been: green, forever-green
tomatoes, incapable of blush, anorexic peas, sticks of zukes,
or just their purple & orange blooms, skimpy & fruitless.
Unlikely gardener I am anyway, over-fond of weeds,
unable to discern invader from guest – will I use
any of this? Then September – late – the sun,
and suddenly, all I had condemned begins to plump,
rouge, swell and, no matter how quickly I pick, more
comes to peak, wagging waste-not digits at my gathering,
so though I bake & give away & cook & eat
raw of the plant's heat – the feast! Yes, of course,
in all those human ways, I fail the feast.

Fall Equinox

Overnight, gold.
A breeze anticipating bareness
as the first shudder of leaves
spatter on yesterday's summer
lawn, leftover vegetables clench
against themselves, un-pickable
now, and the air pinches
like salt in lungs that will soon
need to accustom themselves
to breathlessness.
You can never prepare,
only witness.
Overnight, to our season's longest sonnet,
the turn.

Premonitions in March

Of my six gardens, four, at least, will fail.
One too intimate with weeds my heart can't pull;
A second too much in the shade.
The third? It's full of plants from tenants past.
And the fourth will simply falter, though why I cannot tell.

And of the two that may succeed?
Not if it rains or blasts our heat to tropic heights.
Not if its gardener has to leave.
No, these two also (it must be said) will fail.
I say all this amid tall drifts of snow.

Pantoum of the Wettest July

You can't maintain the sunshine again
Yard apples go Kathunk, Kathunk
Two moths mate on a random grass blade
The wasp nest keeps accreting

Yard apples go Kathunk, Kathunk
Dill rises tall as a small child
The wasp nest keeps accreting
A dragonfly whoops over the chives

Dill rises tall as a small child
Parsley elaborates, basil goes blah blah blah
A dragonfly whoops over the chives
Foxgloves, tiger lilies follow peonies to the stage

Parsley elaborates, basil goes blah blah blah
O now it's three moths in a ménage of weeds
Foxgloves, tiger lilies follow peonies to the stage
Our food is being strangled by beauty

O now it's three moths in a ménage of weeds
The candelabras of apples hang hard and low
Our food is being strangled by beauty
Storms turn the pages of summer too fast

The candelabras of apples hang hard and low
Green reels in its many squirming shades
Storms turn the pages of summer too fast
You can't maintain the sunshine again

Mistakes already made in the garden by May 5th

Got over-eager.
Planted too early.
At least two tomatoes, two strawberries, and three beans may suffer.
Didn't half & half mix in planting the roses.
Were the holes deep enough?
Not likely.
Perhaps the bushes are too far from the trellis.
How many coffee grounds for the blueberries?
Crushed a few squash seedlings.
Dropped too many carrot seeds in one square foot of dirt.
The borders aren't even.
The compostable pots aren't composting.
Did I cut off a beetle's wings by digging too vigorously?
The sunflowers can't get enough sun by the side fence.
Grass keeps pushing back in.
Put too much mulch on everything because it looked nice.
Was that fertilizer the right kind?
Being too random in my planting, too anxious.
How much will survive regardless.
If I say failure, does the garden reply – forgiveness?

May Snow, redux

We rush to canvas up the plants
knowing we've already faltered.

Seeded, as usual, too soon.
But when, in this land, is one sure?

If not snow such as this tip, damp
and blanched stabbings of flakes

dumping all evening and into the night,
sliding in soft plods off the metal roof, then

a choke of rain or wind cracking the heads
off everything. The harsh north is nothing new

but I'm still a child in it, demanding no,
I'm done, never again, while it whites down

on our plans, we slathering the sprouts
with insufficient tarps, cherry blossoms sifting.

Legacy

Now, dreaming of a little orchard,
I begin with one tree,
a Crimson Passion cherry, flitted
with white flowers.

Digging a hole twice the root bole,
I stake it to the earth,
which is both rich and laced
with plastic bits – a modern cradle –

and every time I see its mapped
bark and glint of leaves
I think of Robinson Jeffers,
the 2000 trees he planted

around Tor House, in Carmel,
and though few remain –
I know, I know –
it's the act that matters.

An Abecedarian for the Garden

Alas I know so little about gardening
Because, raised by busy parents in the suburbs,
Crops were mostly bean sprouts on the countertop, yet
Digging is cathartic and once you gouge out a square,
Earth's muck beneath the useless grass, you may as well
Flick a few easy seeds from their bright packets, your
Ground rich, raddled with plastic bits, dreams, not
Harvests, just a ripple of fierce green tips
Inching. On the prairies they say don't plant before May, but
June could also be nippy with slush, or hard rains that
Kill all the full sun needs. Little ambition, mostly
Love – of beauty – sends you to greenhouses, garden centres, to
Mail-ordering trees that arrive as freeze-dried sticks,
No hope they will soon yield. A putterer, you're
Open to positing, randomness, seeing what happens when,
Posing what ifs to the soil, weather, location, engaged in slow
Queries. The former owners planted bitter cukes, a thatch of irises,
Red tomatoes that stayed green in downpours, became
Spectral by fall – mainly, they built raised boxes, then moved.
The now is up to you. What remains, what you're quickly
Uncovering mixed with decisions regarding future
Visions – happy accidents, imagined glories and the ever-present
Weeds you cannot pull, entirely, drawn always to the free and wild amid
Xanthisma's spiky blooms, a plot of broccoli, peas in their twisting climb,
Yarrow against the dandelion, perhaps some carrots, two shades of kale,
Zinnias down every border, the generosity of zucchinis and (why not?) a rose.

Tally in June

One cedar has died.
Two are browned
by the heat or cold
or something in between.
Of four bean plants,
only one survives,
of potatoes, two flourish
but two also refuse the light.
The kale appears to thrive
but one tomato vine
has been tried twice
in the same spot.
Perhaps now it may live.
Peas are mostly reaching.
Basil is good. The second
dill is fine but not one
of the carrots has shown,
the plot bare as a book
with only weed-scrawl
for a story.
No roses at all
but the cherry
anticipates red, there's one
pale strawberry, and as for
the infant apple trees,
there are nubs,
soft promises of fruit.

Tally in July

The peonies have finally expired,
rain hurtling blooms
into petals, or they withdrew
inside dryness, browned fists.
Three miraculous carrots
feather upwards.
Many raspberries; a few strawberries;
no blueberries and the cherries
show the likelihood of fall.
I didn't know potatoes possessed
such delicate flowers, hued
golden & purple as happy old women.
No peppers or cukes.
Some beans suggest themselves.
The herbs have peaked.
Tomatoes: green.
Who knows about the peas.
For weeks now – kale!
Washed in salads, baked into chips –
so much it seems we haven't
picked at all.
There will be squash.
The broccoli spindled into yellow sprays,
collapsed on the lawn in the latest storm:
unlikely.
But for one.
Yet finally the peonies, lovely, domineering,
have died and beneath them –
roses!

Tally in August

The roses are going.
Peas, beans soften, shrivel.
Squash harden, relinquish a few to the oven.
A regular sun has still not rushed the tomatoes.
Between feared stalks of creeping bellwood,
marigolds, pansies continue to push.
One sunflower splays, bees circumnavigate;
others remain sealed.
Only a hand of carrots; a few stubs of cukes;
endlessly, many frayed bushels of kale.
In that last rain, all the potato plants keeled,
a slug traversed the basil, the dill collapsed.
Raspberries shrink inside themselves
as tiny chandeliers of strawberries plump.
The cherries, of course, have been thieved,
blueberries never appeared.
And yes, it will be years until apples happen.

Tally in September

Roses? No more of those.
It's sunflower season now,
though most are stunted or
hunch their thick spines low.
The harvest continues – a further
anticlimax of carrots, eight fingers of beans,
a few curves of peas, maybe three cukes.
Strawberries remain sluggish but raspberries
seem a forever crop, snagging stragglers
by the side gate.
The most successful plant, kale, we've
all wearied of, stopped ripping its leaves for salad
and just let it bush out, a forest for chickadees.
Three squash so far and twelve blooms more?
Promising.
The first potatoes have been pulled, possibly
80 small to mid-sized orbs, two conjoined
like a soft victory sign, multiple circles mobiled,
stones caught in kelp, the yanked plant
trailing its veils all over the yard to where
a choir of tomatoes hold their one green note
as long as they can.

Tally in October

No icicles yet or snow
more than slight flakes
and only the skin of the fountain
ponds have frozen but
the garden?
The garden is done, the last
harvest accomplished:
three green trapezoids of squash
amid dozens of unripened others,
stilted on shrunken vines,
tomatoes that never reddened
now rowing windowsills,
kites of misshapen potatoes yanked
out of the minus soil, tiny
broccolinis spat from a giant plant
and at least a palm of wizened raspberries.
That's all.
Mulch around the small trees.
Hope.

Crabapples

The worst, I first met them
as a brown mush midden in the far
corner of the wobbly yard, unpicked windfall
every August, two trees full of inedible

green nubs that tipped off
at a touch and seemed useless excess,
an irritant under the mower, rendering
that part of the garden impossible to plant

or sit in, the elderly neighbour's bane.
Then the time came, two years on, where I
laddered up and nabbed some for the colander
before the breezes did, found a recipe from a 100-

year-old cookbook for crabapple muffins,
loaded the batter with sugar and maple syrup
and found, though they browned instantly when cut,
in fact appeared rotten prior to being ripe,

they still tasted delicious when baked, tart
slabs of soft forgotten things, and as I ate
the hot fresh baking heard, beyond the lilac bush,
that small battery of apples I hadn't snagged go

thonk, thonk, thonk, in the un-recordable storm,
onto the ground.

Dragonflies

In the garden, one lit upon my face.
Am I the water source?
I'm not the insects that it eats,
its feet lifting at high speeds
in even backwards flight;
and it rarely rests on flowers –
more fence slats, the umbrella's arch.
Have I become an inhuman place
in its 300-million-year-old blood?
This morning I feel my fullest use
as nothing else but this – its mullioned
wings stilled on my cheek in the swift
prairie light and interpreted as forgiveness,
change, a kind of grace.

Reciprocity

The ant checks on the seams of the peony,
the tight, bisecting folds, that globe of tectonic softness.

We see it as sentry or pacer, useless perambulator,
but it's precise, patterned, devotee.

Soon it will pass the task to bees who gather
the honey beneath. They are temporary,

you see, feeders on glints of sugar the bud's
geography yields. And in turn, they fend.

Thrips unfound as the ants pass over paths of sweetness,
guarding the carpel within.

Layers

This – what being a poet is –
        a line arriving in the blood over the course
of a quotidian breakfast

an allegiance to peonies

and that need to repeat and repeat
        until you can return to pen & paper
and write it down – this urgency first, then also,

the truth in how you've spent June attending
        each opening bud to its end where,
within the core of these loosened petals,

you can witness an alien star.

Four Words

April 29, 2021

A construction, a dance, a sedge, a flight
The annual migration of cranes returns
from late in the day to the start of night

You hear their call before catching the sight
of those thousands of wings in a world that churns
with a construction, a dance, a sedge, a flight

Crossing all borders without taking fright
at divisions, resistance, a fear that now learns
from late in the day to the start of night

that hunting and habitat loss is a fight
for all of us equally, each in our turn
That construction, that dance, that sedge, that flight

must be freed in its flow, left to its right
to inhabit its nesting grounds, all that it's earned
from late in the day to the start of night

You hold your head back to the sky as those bright
red-crested cranes bring their beauty that burns
from late in the day to the start of night
A construction, a dance, a sedge, a flight.

The Third Garden

The weeds are getting sneakier.
A poplar's pert propellers seeding in every
garden bed this year, particularity nixed.

Clover, of course, with its sprays of lucklessness,
grass like little jabs from the netherworlds of dirt.
There are always unrecognizable others too, clothed

in the garb of the planted, the wanted.
The green chives are unabashed again, perhaps
a gift once, now flagstone uprooters, inedible.

And the dandelions, inevitably, win the award
for most successful. Mowed or plucked (never sprayed),
they squawk back up overnight: yellow, then the essential

puff that, if you touch, merely bursts into a thousand
more blooms you can't control.
O gardener of the shortest season, let go.

Eternal Recurrence

Dommed by sparrows in the late
September garden, a century of them

on the sunflowers, tugging at the corollas
in their shrivelled hoods of once-bloom,

now a storehouse of circular-stacked seeds.
All winter they will feed on this crop's

sprouted clocks, a yellow matched still
by the heat, then in a hue's certain relief

from the snow, even when brown,
not gold and their petals, those leaves,

slack as arrowed platters, are fixed
beneath the ice like fossils from the recent past,

the sparrows will manifest one kind of eternity.

The Human Nest

Part One

Hardly a heart a-thump on the hot
pavement, barely de-egged, a hatchling
descended from some invisible twigged
hands, a woundless wound.

*

Placed in the palm, eyes unsighted,
just the body's throb, fine etchings
of would-be wings, scritches of pinions,
a melancholic yellow mouth, sealed.

*

Find a box fast, line it with a shred of shirt,
snitched from the garage, the underside
of grass clumps, dried to tired gold,
approximating. Place it beyond your flawed warmth.

*

Stick it in a tree-nook to see if the parents return,
its peeping a seepage. Seek out a small dropper
and pop a drip or two in the beak now open
far too wide for nothingness.

*

There is nothing else to do. Night slits
through and at first light it barely shudders
at touch, too sapped by shock to want.
You won't look again for a while.

Part Two

The end was almost victorious, then not.
Researching how to feed it you lift its box
down from the cedar at intervals of thirty

minutes or so, its clown beak yawed around
the syringe of liquid, then miniscule tweezers
of cat kibble, soaked and dripped with syrup

to a soft beige pulp. Its bald head seized inside
your hold and to gulp it had to convulse in a strange
dance of sustenance.

We would take it to the clinic soon.
It would be saved and our human failures
vindicated for a moment at least.

Instead, going inside the house to fetch, something,
taking, of course, too long, the box was tilted
on return and no bird in its bed.

Magpie? Crow? None of that mattered.
The feeding was what had killed it as in our absence
its pipping called forth death.

The cloth and hay were tipped. The box flattened.
The birds we hadn't interrupted sang
and now it was close to evening again.

Sunflower, August

The mammoth is its own planet.
Each day, for months, it grows inches, thickens,
its pedicel like obese bamboo, leaves plattering out,
shading tomatoes and peas, quashing the cedar's spread.
Height attained, the fleshy receptacle expands,
florets first petalling within, the whole head
a conjunction of spikes, fortress grin or alien apparition.
Every morning, turning in a different direction,
from the dark seed, already prepared
to breathe in the rays, transform bract into corolla.

*

The mammoth is its own planet or a satellite of seeds, each
lipping from a sepal, an anther, but what is most flagrant,
hard to say: the jungle-vast leaves, trunk ridged as night's
spine or this inflorescence, all the stigmas melded, fastened
in florets, the whole a corolla of twisting always
towards the light.

*

The mammoth is its own planet. Its face uninhabited
by grief. Now, growth peaked, it forms seeds within each
eventual unsealing and release. Its scent a honey-musk
that weighs your leaning towards, your burial in the past.
Redeems it. In part. You've lashed it to the deck as if a siren
on the mast but it never stops widening and, at night, floats over
the lawn, a soft moon in prickly carapace.
Believe that it is beyond you and it is.

The Rasp

The rasp of sparrows on the frosted leaves of all the dead sunflowers –

     a noise I'd never heard – their small claws clinging to the rough

undersides of those face-sized fronds – like a book being read too quickly, a raw

     ladder – the world can still surprise my senses it seems, grief

that never gets waylaid, entirely, by joy – or is it the reverse – I've never

     grown flowers tall enough for them to be a source, a concealment,

to gift me with a new sound for winter.

     *

Tiny taps at infinitesimal doors, dried portals to seeds. Have you heard this sound before?

A thousand sparrows in a small crop of sunflowers, the shrivelled limbs of leaves rattling

as each bird body lands. What you see is death but there is never death entire.

Inside the husks of blooms, a winter's wild food. Afraid sometimes of all their endless

needs or glad to have planted what feeds & feeds.

Sonnet on November 14th

Will you always write about the first snow, that
sudden assemblage of flakes, forever unforeseen,
despite reports, this quick shift to the longest season?

The rush to remove what you wanted
to linger – o you knew but waited until
the white & wet on all the summer's furniture –

then dashed out to store it away, surprised –
so humanly unprepared, in denial, shock.
You wouldn't be given endlessly extended heat,

an absurdly prolonged cycle of growth.
You would wake once more to ice,
the tangible sight of breath.

Yes, you will always, too,
write of the last death.

After a Form by Galway Kinnell that also uses the word Winter in the 4th Stanza

Though it was a city, the trees
leant aspects of their wilderness,
whether full with variants of green, the trees,
or pared back to their hardest witness,
they bracketed our every day, those trees.

Otherwise, we would have been overcome by roads,
the endless, straight, rational lines
making squares of the suburbs, roads
also confounding in traffic circles, off-ramps.
Our minds that meeting of roads & roads.

Then our longest announcer: snow,
sometimes in the almost-mild environs, then slitting
down to cold, so cold it can no longer snow
but the white is fixed as if forever's palette
and every edifice is called snow.

A certain way of establishing winter
in its primacy, a city named after one season,
the longest, the most thorough, winter
arriving in fall and re-arriving in spring,
the least consistent surprise of all: winter.

What insisted we survive? Trees.
In every neighbourhood, the certain roads
carrying leaves & litter, sustaining snow
as all the seasons embodied winter.
Winter imprinting snow on the roads, the trees.

The Garden Diary

for Rachael

For three-quarters of the year it's blank.
No words for how the snow grows, sprouts ice,
melts in its wilt of white over all the beds.
The lines hold silence, a prairie waiting
within a coastal impatience.
Then, from May to October, a scrawl of preparing,
fingering in the seeds, overbuying flowers (others think),
yarding out weeds, queries about watering and, after
the brief lavish of colour, the quick & partial harvest.
The diary only gives five or six short lines
in which to first say nothing, after to write the whole
overwhelming season in small, insufficient script.
But I look back on it to note the happiness
of the "enchanting hibiscus," the world's
"tiniest carrots" (remember not to bother
planting those again!), the rain's lack or excess,
the taste of tomatoes toasty from the vine, the
"green radar" of a sunflower attending.

The Fourth-Year Garden, 2022

"weeds do not hesitate"
AMY CLAMPITT

Assembling itself into a moue of peonies,
tri-hued, the bloom that turns one useless;
only the ants work to unfurl and seed in their parade

down the petalled nub, but also the ragged,
unfigured out veggie patch, its opposite, where
willy-nilly amid the wanted singular spinach

and a trio of zukes is a lax smattering of last
year's kale, un-routed, and even titchy carrots
nixed as pointless, but nil cukes or broccoli,

the actually-planted. Clover huddles around
every edible thing, the rude propellers of insistent
poplar, grass, of course, in randy clumps, and now

the sunflowers, once assented to, have proved
permanent and reckless, meat spilled from sparrows'
beaks leaping from every available earth like unclassifiable

gifts, determined to unlock small sunshines
beneath the new and usual clouds of summer

Green Tomatoes

During the season of green tomatoes
you realize the frost is always assembling its crystals.

You prune the excess from the vine, nudging the red
to hasten, holding the knowledge of last year's frozen fruit,

and still hoping.
The gardener must hope to keep planting

even though the hundred days of summer can be counted
on busted popsicle sticks, chalk figures

on the sidewalk, the tiny punctuation of birds.
Bags & bags of green tomatoes are gifted

to invisible neighbours but there are always
those missed, those that switched to red unseen beneath

the branching flow of nasturtiums and old peonies,
that waited for a mouth or didn't, that were found,

ghosts, in spring.

Lullaby

The old bees are the ones you see in the yard.
Those chosen for the last gathering of pollen
after their other duties are done:
feeding the queen her royal jelly while they scrape by on bread,
mating in the hive, dancing the directions of flowers
: all those patterned tasks.

The old bees pause inside corollas, examine
the fable of stamens.
Soon they will receive the stigmata of gold
upon their bellies & thighs
and then they will fly, one final time,
into the sun.

The Neighbourhood

Postcards from the Archives, 1905

1 *From Strathcona over the North Sask to Edmonton.*

"Just a year since I, arrived in this lonely spot. It is hard to say, when I will see dear,
old Fen again. Not for a long time I fear. [Re]'d your letter yesterday.
Love to all, M"

What you always see first: a silo, a church,
the industrial weight of the place
as if the fresh river were already a tailing pond
and the black & white domiciles, factories
built with bitumen, a dark sludge of making do.

The loneliness is no wonder, even now,
from one edge of melt to the other, and then,
when you left, it was for always, a postmark
beyond the heart's bond to beginnings,
that pact to earn a living, to send
love from an early city with all love's
unreachable history calling.

2 *A summer lightning storm in Edmonton at midnight.*

"Dear Gertie waiting for that letter you said you were going to send. This a view
of the storm wee had the other night. The weather is grate here. By by for know.
J.C.W."

The jagged happiness of that sharp storm.
Over the few downtown buildings:
the clock tower, the bank, a bolt
hits, claws its chalk-yellow fissures,
thin illuminations of heat & midnight,

a place where the weather is "grate"
in mid-summer but the wait grating
for a letter you said you said you said
(the admonishment like thunder)
you were going to send.

Gertie, where is she on this close,
sky-breaking evening, this culmination
of humidity, a clash and then that
hum of aftermath and again
when when when.

No love on this postcard
only the weather, a poor grammar of demands.

3 *Two images of the North Sask River. One featuring the High Level Bridge.*

"Dear Dad. Pattern arrived safely. Many thanks. Will duplicate as soon as possible. Robt."

The still-treed river curve, then one side Strathcona,
the other Edmonton and between, the black steel
of the High Level Bridge, once two directions, now
narrow dual lanes falling a single way across the little-
used, drawn for all water. And what was that pattern
he asked for and received? Given the era, architectural
rather than garb? Curt but thankful, speaking of expediencies,
today, this would be a text, not the faded glamour
of a postcard, silent but implying love, certain
& reliable as the correspondences of river & river.

4 *Some of Edmonton's residences as photographed by C.W. Mathers.*

"Dear Sister, hope you are getting along well. Give Emerson my love.
Bert Harrids"

They built grand immediately, echoes of ostentation,
resonance in bricks of lands mostly lost, left
for the new bleak, a Klondike dream, the chance
to establish, as Mathers himself did with the earliest
photo business in town, when Edmonton
was still part of the Northwest Territories.

Yet, families were never seen again, relations
of the everyday quotidian, allegiances, not formed from speech,
so the wish is simple: wellness, love to likely a child,
sibling formalities amid the pompous absurdity
of mansions set in harsh introductions of mud.

5 *View of a walking path and a footbridge over a creek in a heavily wooded area.*

"Hello Gert. How are you? You are a terrible time in writing. The baby does
better than you. Was that Pauline Middleton again. Clara"

The city was there, somewhere, inside the vast
brush, clot of coyotes and sumac like a pebble
in a kingdom of stone, a seed in a world of forests.

There is only a thin path over this thick creek and
Clara will you walk it? Why will Gert not respond –
is it lack of speed, a dearth of penmanship?

She a baby and you warrior, settler, strangely
concerned about the elusive Pauline, her repetitions.
How are you, you ask, but there is too much

wilderness around it and where's the love
outside this dark postcard – who's still in the parlour
and who's in the mire, who's sipping tea

and who swallows hard draughts of no
going back, inexplicable, impossible, in those
few inked, impassable lines.

Mowing the Ghost House

Every summer, each week, a crew arrives and fast, as though it doesn't
matter, they buzz and zap the front and back
grass of the home on my left.
No one has lived there for years.
In the winter, they return for snow, scraping its epidermis
off walks, clearing the path to the door never exited
nor entered.
The woman who used to live at this address is lost
to illness, relocated elsewhere, the rooms now
run by mice, the dog house dark,
but she still pays for her property to retain the traces
of being human, of holding ownership.
This: all we truly are, a low-cut lawn,
the snow bladed raw.

To the Thief who Reads Poetry

We live in a neighbourhood of roamers, pickers, backyard pissers so
it wasn't even her wandering in Joe and Jane's snowy enclosure
that startled, or her slipping beneath the cedars to pee, it was how
she lied to me once I called – can I help you – as she yanked the back door,

teetered on its rotting sill and claimed to be a granddaughter of the old
couple who lives there – I just forgot my key!
Yet when I asked for her name, she became stranger, closed, refused –
a young girl only, seemingly not sketched out, but obviously not a relation, either.

Then I noticed the book in her hand, a white slab with stark '70s lettering –
Anne Szumigalski's *Woman Reading in Bath* – and almost stopped questioning
her motivations, wanted to let her into the neighbours' with a secret password,
fill the tub high, enable her to honour the title, sink into its surreal dreams.

Poetry being its own thieving after all, its own set of sweet lies, a perfect
disguise against a world that needs you to build fences and say, to almost
everything in the end – you don't belong here and where's your receipt?
And then she fled, the poems of a dead Canadian poet, cynosure, into the streets.

Two Incidents in Pandemic Times

Shoppers Drug Mart on 118th Avenue

Pop

His cart is so cornucopia'd, things ditch
      onto the arrowed floor of Shoppers, the metal maw
stuffed with stacks of pop, layers of bright plastic,
      half-price.
Women, he starts, and there is a shrinking in me from the beginning of time –
      how will he now define, dismiss us, how will he,
like my father back then, make me feel I should have been a boy, or perhaps
      am one?
Women, he continues, *what we do for them,* and I disappear
      as a witness, resist the imprecations, while
acknowledging the need to feel heroic in these men, who have lifted
      so many bottles of Sprite, Coke, solely (it seems)
for the ladies in their lives.
      Women, he finishes, *we carry all their heavy stuff* and I think
of the rape-abortion-loss-sorrows-births inside my gut,
      squatting within my mouth that no man has hefted from the weighed
cart of my body, but ok –
      you have schlepped these items of forgetfulness into the house
so I can drink, drink this false sweetness
      down.

Spray

In the year of the plague, a woman in Shoppers steals – something –
   a minor perfume, a body spray – too pricey for her to purchase –
is caught and at the cash register told to give it back, to leave

it behind. Her mouth is husked in a mask and so when hate spouts out
   it remains inside the small cave of cloth – doesn't but seems to –
the words, *You effing N* . . . addressed to the security guard, who has been calm

& kind, reminding her she is wasting time and should just let it go, should relinquish
   the tiny vial of beauty she can't afford *–You effing N* . . . she yells, spits, but
the rage is muffled by the soft armour across her mouth, the words huddle hard against

her lips, the fabric now visibly damp – is she feeling her anger ricochet back down
   her throat or is her partly-anonymous face making her brave,
brave enough to hate loudly – there are at least four sources of pain here as the store

takes back its product and righteous or sorrowful customers wait in their own
   agony-masks
to pay.

Five Businesses between 118th Ave and Little Italy

1 Fast Shoe Repair

Forty years it's been here, the red stucco proverbial
hole in the wall, wall to wall with leather slabs, rubber
soles, steel machines, shelves of un-picked-up shoes,
a wonky chair by the door to slip on your fixed pair
and a cash box (bills only and not even up front)
on the scarred countertop. Gino used to run it but
retired, finally, to dance, and now Manny from Ghana
has taken over, though he tires already of the cheap,
everyone wanting everything for less and how, he says,
am I to cover the bills, to keep paying for the lights to stay on.

2 Pink Polish Nail Salon

None of them have names we know in that soft
Vietnamese tongue, but their friendliness extends
through the white room with its phalanx of massage
chairs, wall of rainbow-hued bottles, Plexiglass shields,
a TV playing infomercials, the usual stations for feet
and hands and in the back, the secret ministrations of the face.
Always a vague guilt, whether with a shoe shine or pedi,
at participating in a hierarchy of un-absolvable depths,
but one pays to feel good and so, the limb extends,
is scrubbed, trimmed, rubbed and painted, for a time,
a colour that reminds you of youth.

3 Norwood Dental Centre

The dentist of my childhood was like this: about prizes
(though the plastic cowboy & Indian sets have been nixed),
about pleasures (hand-held Frogger then, now Netflix,
vibrating chairs, weighted blankets). This office
even more affable, with its appellations of "friend,"
its offerings of coffees before your root canal, though
in the end, as even the fish in their waiting room tank
may sense, it's still about pain: its relief, its return.

4 Wee Book Inn (shut down in 2020)

There is a cat, of course, that wanders the stacks, plops,
basketed by the till, and the predictable Rod McKuens,
fantasy pulp, self-help tomes. Music bios are their forte,
classic Canadian novels, even forgotten vinyl, and always
the one crony blabbing, the kid trying to snag a buck
off a set of his grandad's Britannicas, the reader who
never purchases, just stands entranced in the aisles, held
by the slow bird-flutter of the pages.

5 Zocalos

A dream of exotic, bright, when melancholic you can just walk
into this world, there will be a ceramic parrot for your sorrow or plants
in tiny pots shaped like turtles, a plethora of lush green, beaten tin
mobiles, fountains, hummingbird stakes for your roses or just –
sit with an apricot beer, a muffin from the sunrise and, amid
other dreamers, those who hold out gardens as hopes, who know
a dose of colour cures – sometimes it's simple to heal awhile
and you will never emerge sadder than you were.

Kingsway Mall, Alberta Avenue, Winter 2023

Hating malls always, no, truly,
since adolescence at least when the labyrinth
was flirty, WH Smith sold books,
Sam the Record Man was only that,
and Orange Julius was our go-to
quencher of thirsts, even then it was
too fluorescent, pressured, repetitive,
the same shoulder-padded shirts
in every store and, around each corner,
soaps or burgers or Swatches at a kiosk.
The dullness blared. Never so tired
as after an era at the mall and yet once
in a while now, forced to enter by a dental
or bank appointment, the lingering isn't
so painful. Between those strolling seniors,
men a-loitering on mathematically-planted
couches, teens of course still shy or snickering,
the thousand languages of the world interlacing
in the adroitly heated air, the stores can
flower out with their dreams of beauty,
flanked by murals, budded by clerks in
their sweet assistance of youth and be
somehow lovely, an awakening, after all.

Mona's Pub, 118th Avenue

for Michelle

In this microcosm, everything:
riches from the dinging slots
or tournaments of pockets, music
in the weekly sing-songs of AC/DC
and Loretta Lynn, sports (mainly
the Oilers), food, well, fried but deals
galore and beer is always cheap and
love? Beyond the once-curb stomps
and shoot-em-ups in sewagey toilet veins,
rarer since management changed, are
the lengthening tables of laughter, bar-
circled flirtations, kisses even from a random
rapper, compliments from older & older men.
The women of mostly mid-life who sling
the drafts and Porn Stars, serve this world
into being: their tender gestures, their fierceness.
The anonymous are now named, the legless lifted
onto stools, the ministry continues, the poison
becomes balm again, the day, night.

New Year's Eve Feast at the Hotel Macdonald, 2018: a sestina for Michael

Nine years on and they seat us where he and I had sat, him
a scraggly man with gangly teeth but still, somehow, a beauty
to me, and you so very different, wearing a shirt of blue koi swimming, you,
on this last day of what had been a strange, victorious year,
yes, both hard and a joy, as in the posh salon of couples and blood
they asked us only one question: who is having the beef, who the lamb?

Now I don't, as a habit, eat much meat, but with ease tonight I choose lamb,
a course that will arrive amid the six, the memory of him
sitting across from me, bursting goofily with grins, blood
continuing ripe in his veins, not flat in its hush before ash, that simple beauty
of being alive and holding hope like a fork in your hand, the long year
before his death, slides tears into my eyes, though you

are the one across from me, un-discountable, odd and lovely gift, you
worker, musician, weeper, pushing up your glasses (that you call goggles), no lamb
for you but short rib thinly shredded, a seared foie gras, grits, thrilled the year
brought us together, you from Winnipeg, I Vancouver, an intro finagled by him?
The ghost? Tough not to think so, he leaving me funds for the house, a heritage beauty,
me renting you a room, asking his image not to leave me lonely, vigorous blood

surging in me, unwilling to live only in remembering's blood,
that heat and sorrow, but wishing for someone to enter the now with, you
equally exuberant, talented, understanding of the artist's erratic life, and a beauty
too (Samurai mask melded with Ferrigno), a human lamb
in a lion's sign, the opposite of what he was, basically that once-him
a fish, slippery even to himself, but quick with love, wanting to grow old, year

after year, with me, yet incapable of enduring the world, his 29th year
his last, ending in an overdose of crack, not, as he imagined, in a wreck's blood,
and no I don't often obsess anymore, think or talk endlessly about him
but tonight he's here, in this 1915 Harvest Room, and of course I tell you
sometime during the wagyu with quail's eggs, the apple nage with caviar, before the lamb
appears, arrayed on its platter like a soft cross with sweetbreads and soy peppers, a beauty

of food I eat with mincing bites because beauty is slow, beauty swells in the mouth, beauty
is in seeing you across from me, also smiling with the delicacies and the happiness this year
has unwittingly delivered, the contrast of plates between us, you the beef, I the lamb,
but in the same space, winkled with lights the hues of emerald, ocean, blood,
Terry the harpist tenderly plucking Nirvana tunes, wine incessantly replenished, and you
near me now with that ache of newness and promise that allows me to forget him,

O only for moments at a time, beauty residing in the mind beyond blood,
the end of this wild year containing both the adorable solidity of you,
the last of the lamb (sorbet to finish) and, as some warm presence, the ghost of him.

Classic Rock Fest, Edmonton Racetrack, with Prism, Glass Tiger and Tom Cochrane

August 11, 2021

Rush the gates with teen verve – few under 40 – almost relishing the bag check,
      the pat-down though we're more likely to be concealing a Chardonnay

in a cooler now, no more mickeys up the snatch. The tables, Cochrane later
      notes, remind him of a field of solar panels or the largest wedding

he's ever played. Short lineups for merch, longer to snag a folding plastic chair
      you better have brought a plush cushion for, longest for the stretched

bay of potties, each with a urinal, hole, sanitizer and a tiny warped door mirror.
      O too close, too close! As always, drinks are overpriced: Coors, Bud Light,

some kind of tropical fruit with gin, ordered online and served at your seat, worse
      are the food trucks where 40 bucks buys you two slabs of vegan lasagna,

no poutine thanks. But does it matter. Music is what we're here for, nostalgia, the stage,
      amps, strobes extra-magical now after months of deprivation. Seated between

a farmer and his shaking-it wife, sporting a chapeau suitable for a royal gala,
      and a couple who look like they're camping, sloped in folding seats

as if the distant show is a fire, water bottles like candles. Prism was throwback
      giddiness; Glass Tiger a brevity of resonance; Tom the perfect Canadian,

apologizing for talking too much, singing fully from a renegade heart, jigging
      like your happy Dad. The heat was mostly grit; to dance, at first, was wheezy but,

eventually, dusk, a slight breeze and solo on the sapped grass, the music entered me,
      not just in a bygone sense but from now's need to move – a power in this urge –

time live as its moment's wires, acres of unaccustomed dancers upon a disused racetrack
      and the sun and the floodlights passing each other on the ways they were going –

up, down, up, down.

Together Again Festival at the Edmonton Racetrack with Danko Jones, I Mother Earth and Our Lady Peace

August 28, 2021

Is there a hierarchy of fans here – those who dance (few) and those who
mouth the lyrics, purchase shirts warning us against the Stupid Famous, or
ignore all performers as if in a living room of phones & popcorn (too many to note).

Danko suggests, "You would enjoy it more on your feet," but to the New Wave
proggers from Mars this is merely Neanderthal logic, glancing askance at fist-
popping, braid-twirling beats while honing their geeky, immovable coolness.

Danko thanks Charlie Watts, recently deceased; the others offer up Cohen,
Neil Young, a Gord Downie tribute, taut with congas, tambourines amid
the usual instruments as screens inflict their faces, slightly aged, still-fierce,

upon a thousand tables arrayed with donairs & beer, water & sunscreen.
The dark dips harder near autumn and before nine we are a field of shapes
waving electronic flashlights in small parodies of past flames.

Drunker now, inclined to heckle or yell Encore, a mass
of humans even secretly wanting to feel – needing to believe
this – and music the passage of our yearning.

A Revolving Sestina on The Stadium Tour, 2022, Commonwealth Stadium, Edmonton

In the house, the beastmaster of nostalgia.
You can't fathom the thronging crowds,
as if the whole world had become old,
even the teens, here to witness the lights,
dressed in jester-fashion, black & red,
steaming in the stadium's cauldron, the heat

thick with early-September fires, a heat
that admits no breath, the sun a red
thwack spinning off steel rails, the bleachers' glass all lights
as Joan Jett kicks into hits, those never-old
repetitions of runaways & clover, cherry bombs & jukeboxes, crowds
pouring down to the floor, intent on nostalgia's

renewal, the way it claims your youth was valid, nostalgia
a stamp of history's approval and now, before the clotting crowds,
Poison sings of roses, their glam looks discarded, old,
replaced by sump-pump jam space memories, lights
of a final gratitude, a tribute to Eddie's white & red
guitar, the stage and its wild, eternal heat,

while the audience steeps in the night's extended heat,
snagging merch from the snake-lines, skin so red
from hours of waiting, yet when Def Leppard lights
the stage, you forget everything, the nearly-old
reality of Joe's silver hair, how tracks are crowds
of excess sound, as Let It Go slides you into nostalgia's

eliding arms, the songs repeating 13's nostalgia
to you, how every word clenched rebellion's crowds
of acts you could manifest, in theory, how old
would never happen to you, within the toggling lights
of your private makeup mirror, the endless blush, applied red
on cheeks that needed nil embellishment, that heat

of hunger deepened by Mötley Crüe's discovery, a bad-boy heat,
so that now, 38 years after first seeing their black & red
logo, they remain, in your weird sky, persistent lights,
Vince slipping up on lyrics, too many girls & strobes, Mick old,
but you, in this endless, intense instant, meld with the screaming crowds,
and whether this nostalgia is a kind of mental rot, nostalgia's

stupid lights in the gut, it feels red as happiness, its heat
never old, all the recollections crowds of hell-yeah nostalgia.

Rock the District with Carole Pope, Helix, Harlequin and Loverboy, June 2023

O Edmonton, festival city, so intent on celebration beyond
the long winter that another concert is offered downtown
during June, our new monsoon season.

O Canada flag-spattered ponchos a-bob like jellyfish
on Mars in the parking lot turned venue as the bands
from retro-land spin their forever-hits.

O Helix, fave adolescent act still turning me 15
with fist-pumps and screams as Vollmer poses, struts, extends
the aura of rock star, writ small, our Heavy Metal Cowboy.

O Damp Sandwich returned to in a sodden camping chair,
the downpour double-kicking the asphalt, that definite
joy of the elements disassembling you, and the music, always.

Ed: a sonnet

Blues on Whyte, 2019

Recognizable as the Wild West, Ed,
in his black cowboy hat, stocky silver buckles, tall
and bearded as John Berryman at the end, never
vacates the dance floor the whole of Saturday afternoon,
the Commie bopping with seniors shaking like a field
of slow daisies, Ed the one gyrating his thin hips,
gripping the bar where his near-empty Heineken
trembles or going down for a deep squat in the middle
of it all, ringed fingers revolving their tipsy peace signs,
unable to stop moving for a minute, except when
he passes by to tell me that two years ago he nearly
jumped from the High Level Bridge but bought a
guitar instead and wow was that a good decision
that has saved him every day and every other day, since.

Cook County Saloon, October 2020

for Michael

Ten months since you've greased a stage, serving
as side guy bassist for country bands (mainly, this
being the prairies), seven months of plague
annulments and the show resumes, with its Hell
Yeahs and Devils going down to Georgia, its women
with crimped bangs and men in cowboy or ball lids,
checked shirts, boots that click when they two-step.
Except they can't do that yet – dance – and the crowd
is limited to a century of bodies set apart in table zones,
asked to wear masks. Still, even faced with the echo of death,
the flesh rarely feels like stillness, and couples whirl in their
own worlds, a birthday girl tilts against the barricade until
the singer squats down for a pic, and o those shots keep coming,
riding to the stage on their trays, Smokey cradling his steel
guitar, the Newfie dusting the drums hard and you moving
behind the bass as you otherwise resist, kicks patterning out
the rare beauty of this night.

Pandemic Road Trips, 2020

[take one]

1. Driving

The streets are mostly stricken. As if from a ledger, I mean, crossed out
as thoroughfares of commerce, their stores stating Closed until Further Notice
or simply boarded up or dark. There is nowhere to stop but one gas station where
the cashier (in mask & gloves) allows us to use the sad bathroom for the price of one pack
of Mr Peanuts. Apart from this, we spot a bison's head in a ditch, and from a rig,
the tattooed driver nods at me and – almost – I feel young for a moment, as if touch
with a stranger were still possible in the world.
And then we, simply, keep going.

2. Alberta Beach

The summer town is shuttered, of course. But even more so now: the children's church sealed
and Mom's Diner only open for takeout of meatball sandwiches and cheese casseroles.
April but the lake is solid and a new snow flicks down.
We stand on the rim of nothingness, figures against a universe of white mist & ice.
Distance is easy here at least, no one thinks to enter what is left us.

3. Beechmount Cemetery

Probably the best place to hang out – the dead contain no viruses deep beneath
the earth and their stones are disinfected with snow. There is nobody here
visiting absence.

4. Emily Murphy Park

Picking up quick burgers from a ghosted drive-thru, we walk the trail from
the stalled bridge construction to the stump where woodpeckers & chipmunks converge.
People we pass have scarves bandaged over their mouths, seem to have slipped
away from pleasantries, except for one old man who calls through the cold, "Such a beautiful
day, isn't it?" And we assent. As it was.

[take two]

1. Bison

Heading east towards Lloydminster on Easter – as usual –
the closures, the Ukrainian village boarded up, Elk Island National Park denying
visitors the solace of the forest and those snowy plains where – wow,
a whole clump of bison mowing down on damp grasses!
We dash through snowbanks to somehow access their majesty but end up only
with wet knees, two whitetail deer skittering off
as those mythy silhouettes stir their shagginess away.

2. The World's Largest Pysanka

Breathtaking & symbolic as the website promises (though visitors
are generally less generous in their assessments), this slowly spinning egg
on its metal pedestal, thirty-some feet high, emblazoned with hundreds of stars
in the colours of harmony (constructed for the RCMP in 1974 using an unheard-of
computer model) is, well, an unavoidable attraction (the only one?) in Vegreville.
Having seen the largest perogy in Glendon, the egg was inevitable, even
at a time when Baba's stand is shut, the toilets locked, the only other people
a Mennonite couple who look fast and leave, the wind stinging here,
the egg a hard memory of festivals and less fear.

[take three]

1. Sunglasses

At a St. Albert Shell station, I succumb to the sharpened rays of spring, seeking
a cheap pair of shades from a rack I realize could be layered with contaminants,
popping a few on my face fast, selecting the least scratched twenty-dollar option.
Cash? The cashier asks with trepidation, a slight horror perhaps, as I lay the bills
down that selling a poetry book has brought me. A blue-gloved hand plonks
my change on the counter outside the wide glass partition that now seems permanent.
Have a nice day no longer so accurate a farewell.

2. Beer

He, aiming to obtain Sapporos for our short stops, likely in parking lots, is informed
a hack on the government source has led to a shrunken supply.
An additional indignity of first-world yearnings for sure.
Reduced to sipping Pabst in fields drowned by thaw.

3. Morinville & Bon Accord

Settled by Scots as early as 1892, established by Pere Morin whose brick St. Jean Baptiste
church lives on along with other old-world edifices, the aesthetics of an eternal England
in the middle of the prairies. I want to look at trees in the nursery on the edge of town but
of course it's shut and besides, only mud still as the melt just started last week.
Always overeager for the impossible, me. We turn back on knuckled roads, drive
behind trucks stickered with anti-Trudeau circles, x-ed out hammers and sickles.
The Rednex Pub sign continues to glow. Much later, the settlement of Bon Accord,
that old country motto, now known for its Dark Skies initiative, a stunted clock tower,
a tiny library whose marquee encourages us to adventure in books
while the wild is denied us – not much else. We don't stop.
There's no biggest this or that to snap a pic of anyway.
Except the wrecked Stegosaurus of a faded grain elevator, grim
against the new witness of clouds.
We air band to Mötley Crüe's *Greatest Hits* all the short way home.

[take four]

1. Ma-Me-O Beach

Thinking we saw the last holdouts of ice sliding down the North Sask
on our short hike prior, we were somewhat shocked at how Pigeon Lake at Ma-Me-O Beach
(founded in 1924, Cree for many-shore-birds though we saw none) was still so white,
snow alternating with mud and the whole sphere shades of blue ice.
That vast witness feeling. We sought it on the edges of all.

2. On forgetting to go into Lacombe but instead finding Dalby Cemetery

These days, destinations are mostly redundant. Pick one on a map
then go anywhere else on the way. Falun with its churches, cows, a Mexican
food outlet for bikers. A bottle depot in the middle of fields.
Battle River shushing beneath the land, its barns tilted sideways like time.
Then you see the sign – Dalby Cemetery – and we stop. The first grave from 1914 –
one Per Asp and his wife; the latest, Gail, Doreen or Noreen waiting to join their men.
Markers carved with long-haul trucks, sewing machines, a guitar, a hammer.
We rearrange the wind's rearrangement of plastic blooms then piss on the rim of the plots
where the graves have long conceded to weeds and shrubs and cattle murmur at us.
When we finally arrive in Lacombe, we're only hungry for a fast burger, then turn
back at the World's Biggest Fishing Lure, and head home.

Elk Island, July 2020

An almost-myth clod-hops across the road,
ungulate of history's silhouette –

that shaggy shape grazing in the knob & kettle
field, transcending its near-extinct fright.

People, stuffed in the back of pickup trucks,
scarf their sandwiches, watch through lenses.

Nearby, on small Astotin Lake, scurfed with foam,
nearly luminous with algae, children from all countries

ravage each other's sandcastles, some sporting
masks against the recent plague, all with creams & caps

to shield them from the cranked sun. Stay close,
the parents warn. How we kill to the brink

of absence, then gather in, gather in.

Kelley's Bathtub, Jarvis Lake, Hinton, AB

for Katherine

The sand – scruffy.
A girl in a swipe of a bikini swims with a large, scared dog.
An old lady – miserable as Hagar – gripes, "This is a place of leashes!"

Everything is inflatable: fat families grow fatter during picnics,
unicorns & flamingoes & donuts plump themselves in the shallows,
there are no photos snapped without ameliorating filters.

Beauty is squandered on humans.
The crisp waters offer some momentary happiness, a breeze
shudders through most sorrows, a sliding of sun makes even

the rudest of my scars bearable. Then
I notice the sad things. Above the minnowed surface, a moth
folds into a soft boat; loons further their silences in the smoke.

Poets are awful people.
There is no possible sufficiency for us.

The Taxidermist's B & B, Hinton, AB

What could be more human.
Sometimes it's this simple.
A wall of animals, posed in their lost environments: a ram

with prickly pears, bear poised in approximations of salal,
the mountain goat holding its posture on a slab of stone
affixed to the high-beamed roof.

Everything is thought out.
You can't say it's not beautiful.
Even if you hate death for other than the essential, or survival, or accident.

Despite glass eyes, each remains present: a flicker of hairs
on an under-lip, the velvet still streaming off a set of antlers,
their established majesty.

They watch us, whether alive or dead,
or they remain indifferent.
We play pool beneath them;

we cook small parts of a cow;
we make love with intelligent machines.
A lynx, stilled and celebrated in its fierceness

arches from a branch; bones swirl us into their artful vortex.
We are seen by everything and no one.
The emptied woods hold to snow.

Lines at Drumheller, Oct 31, 2021

for Chris

Geese, engines of sunrise, separate from their reflections, raucous
        letters over the Red Deer River.

Twenty years since I met you; nearly twelve years gone.
        Not lonely. Not alone, but still in wonder at how

you aren't here, remembering your clear face in the Badlands shadows
        as you basted my birthday steak over a solemn fire.

All these moments that reappear as I shift landscapes.
        The same ancient place reminding and reminding, that wheeling

back to the water to say hello once more before flying
        fast into the day again.

Coda: The Fine Print

This was something you didn't consider –
that even though you can love enough to make
things bearable, beautiful – a house, a human –
that through their presence shining the new
prairie world like a snow-sun globe on your mind's
shelf – you can still feel – bereft – a castoff from a land
that, in your child-brain, was yours: trees, salt, the heights
of Grouse and Seymour, all those names you didn't know
were dominance; and a dollar that kept rising until staying
was a felled delusion – you remember that once-dream
of a simple cabin on a wild island and you the forever-forager,
dweller within a coastal bond – and laugh – though you want
to weep – it was something unconsidered – the wrench,
an emptiness at the centre of all decisions – to shift from
the known, to say it doesn't matter or, another place
can supplant when – for the rest of your life – you will
have to hold both now, carry two buckets: BC & Alberta,
and you the teetering fulcrum, an impossible inhabitant
of witness-grasses, chains of waves, each weighing
on your shoulders, or heart, or other parts you didn't –
in innocence, haste, blindness – imagine would be factors –
and you didn't consider – did you – the ghosts.

Coda: Home, 2018–2023

Five years here and though the salt will always
        sing in me, that landscape of trees, sea, plushed-out, towering,

unfathomably grand as natural pianos in a marbled topography,
        taking orders from the heart to perform, even if only in dreams,

when I'm there, the yearning for my dirt overpowers, those patches of raddled
        earth where, planting the seeds of this & that, home accrues,

articulates, and when the whole panoply opens: colour, books, music, cats, the senses
        are enveloped in the now made mortar, gable, essential foundation,

yes, even to the fissures where nests begin.

Acknowledgements

Thank you to the Alberta Foundation for the Arts, who awarded this manuscript a project grant in 2021.

The following poems in this collection were previously published: "An Abecedarian for the Garden" in Pinhole Poetry, "Six Words" in Stonecrop, "Sunflower, August" and "Getting There" in Recovering Words, "Four Words" in Blue Unicorn, "Seasonal Pantoum, Slightly Tinged" in Event, and "Pantoum of the Wettest July" in Freefall. Thank you to the editors.

Other Books by Catherine Owen

Somatic: The Life and Work of Egon Schiele
The Wrecks of Eden
Shall: ghazals
Cusp / detritus
Dog (with Joe Rosenblatt)
Frenzy
Seeing Lessons
Catalysts: Confrontations with the Muse
Trobairitz
Designated Mourner
The Other 23 and a Half Hours or Everything You Wanted to Know
    that Your MFA Didn't Teach You
The Day of the Dead
Dear Ghost,
Riven

Catherine Owen, from Vancouver, BC, has published sixteen collections of poetry and prose, including *The Wrecks of Eden* (Wolsak and Wynn, 2002), *Frenzy* (Anvil Press, 2009), *Designated Mourner* and *Riven* (ECW, 2014 and 2020). Her work has won the Stephan G. Stephansson Prize, been translated into Italian and toured Canada twelve times. She now edits, tutors, and hosts the podcast Ms Lyric's Poetry Outlaws from Delilah, her 1905 home in Edmonton, AB.